AMAZING SCIENCE

Air

Outside, Inside, and All Around

Written by Darlene R. Stille
Illustrated by Sheree Boyd

Special thanks to our advisers for their expertise:

Paul Ohmann, Ph.D., Assistant Professor of Physics
University of St. Thomas, St. Paul, Minnesota

Raymond Hozalski, Ph.D., Associate Professor of Environmental Engineering
University of Minnesota, Minneapolis

Susan Kesselring, M.A., Literacy Educator
Rosemount-Apple Valley-Eagan (Minnesota) School District

PICTURE WINDOW BOOKS
MINNEAPOLIS, MINNESOTA

Managing Editor: Bob Temple
Creative Director: Terri Foley
Editor: Nadia Higgins
Editorial Adviser: Andrea Cascardi
Copy Editor: Laurie Kahn
Designer: John Moldstad
Page production: Picture Window Books
The illustrations in this book were prepared digitally.

Picture Window Books
151 Good Counsel Drive
P.O. Box 669
Mankato, MN 56002-0669
1-877-845-8392
www.picturewindowbooks.com

Printed in the United States of America.

Library of Congress Cataloging-in-Publication Data
Stille, Darlene R.
Air : outside, inside, and all around / written by Darlene Stille ;
illustrated by Sheree Boyd.
v. cm. — (Amazing science)
Includes bibliographical references and index.
Contents: The air around you—What's in air?—Feeling air—
Air and weather—Keeping air clean—Experiments—Airy facts.
ISBN-13: 978-1-4048-0248-3 (hardcover)
ISBN-10: 1-4048-0248-7 (hardcover)
ISBN-13: 978-1-4048-0346-6 (softcover)
ISBN-10: 1-4048-0346-7 (softcover)
1. Air—Juvenile literature. [1. Air.]
I. Boyd, Sheree, ill. II. Title. III. Series.
QC161.2 .S75 2004
551.5—dc22
                                                    2003016444

Table of Contents

The Air Around You

A kite soars on a windy spring day. Tree branches sway. A cloud floats across the sky.

Air is all around you. You cannot see air, but you can feel it. Wind is moving air. It blows in your hair. It pushes a sailboat across a lake.

FUN FACT

All animals and plants need air to stay alive. A person can live several days without food but only a few minutes without air.

Wrap yourself up in a blanket. The earth is wrapped in a blanket, too. The earth's blanket is made of air. This blanket of air is called the atmosphere.

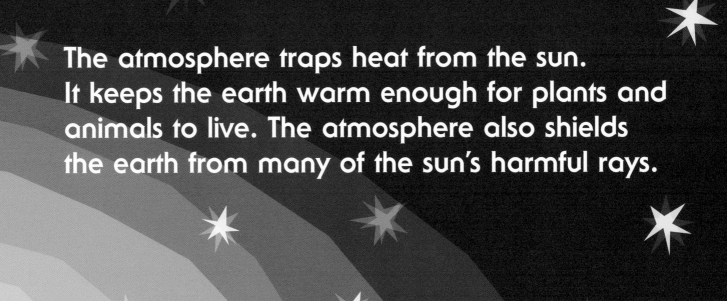

The atmosphere traps heat from the sun.
It keeps the earth warm enough for plants and
animals to live. The atmosphere also shields
the earth from many of the sun's harmful rays.

FUN FACT

Near the earth, the atmosphere
is thick. It gets thinner the higher
up you go. Test pilots flying up
high must carry their own air in
special tanks. They breathe this
air through masks and hoses.

What's in Air?

Take a deep breath. Feel air filling your lungs. Air is made of gases.

One gas in air is called oxygen. Oxygen is important for life. Animals breathe in oxygen. Plants give off oxygen.

FUN FACT

Oxygen goes into your lungs when you breathe. Your blood carries this oxygen to all parts of your body. The oxygen helps give you energy to play soccer, climb stairs, and do everything else throughout your day.

Breathe out. Push air from your lungs. One of the gases you're breathing out is called carbon dioxide. It is another important gas in air. Plants use carbon dioxide to make their food.

NOT-SO-FUN FACT

Carbon dioxide is one of the gases that traps heat from the sun. Scientists worry that people are putting too much carbon dioxide into the earth's air. This carbon dioxide comes from burning wood, coal, gas, and oil. Too much carbon dioxide could make the earth too hot.

In the morning you can
feel dew on the grass.
It makes your feet wet.
Where does it come from?

Dew comes from water vapor.
Water vapor is another gas
in air. When water vapor
cools, it becomes tiny drops
of water.

FUN FACT

Water vapor that cools high up in the air makes clouds. Fog and mist come from water vapor, too. Fog is a cloud near the surface of the earth. Mist is a thin fog.

Feeling Air

Wave your hand in front of you. What feels like a breeze is the air rubbing against your hand.

FUN FACT

Air resistance makes heat. Sometimes chunks of metal or stone fall from space. As they fall toward the earth they rub against air. Air resistance makes the falling chunks hot enough to burn. The burning chunks are called meteors. Most of them burn up before they reach the ground.

Air rubs against speeding cars and planes the same way. This air rubbing against a car, a plane, or your hand is called air resistance.

Take a ride in an elevator.
You can feel your ears pop.
Your ears pop because
of changes in the air.

Air pressure is the weight of air pushing down on the earth. There is more pressure closer to the ground than higher up. The air pressure in the elevator goes down as you go up, but the air pressure inside your ears stays the same. When air pops out of your ears, the air pressure inside your ears becomes the same as the pressure outside.

Fun Fact

It may be hard to think of air as weighing anything. You don't usually feel air's weight because it's pressing on you from all sides. Believe it or not, the weight of the atmosphere on your shoulders is about one ton.

Air and Weather

Have you ever seen a hot air balloon go up? Fire heats the air inside the balloon. The hot air is lighter than the cooler air around it. It makes the balloon float into the sky.

Hot air always goes up. Cold air always sinks. Air moving up and down makes the wind blow.

FUN FACT

Did you ever wonder why it's so windy by an ocean or lake? Air over land heats up faster than air over water. The warm air rises. Cool air over the water rushes in over the shore. The breeze feels good when you are on the beach.

19

Keeping Air Clean

Yucky things can get into the air. Smoke from cars and factories can make the air dirty and smelly. Things that should not be in the air cause air pollution. People work hard to keep the air clean.

Take a deep breath. Think about the air around you.
Now you know that air is made of many things.

Experiments

Make a Barometer

A barometer tells when air pressure is rising or falling. Changing air pressure means there could be a change in the weather.

What you need:
scissors
a round rubber balloon
a small jar or soup can
a rubber band
a drinking straw
tape or glue
a sheet of paper
a pen

What you do:
1. Make sure you have an adult to help you.
2. Cut off the open end of the balloon with the scissors.
3. Stretch the balloon over the mouth of the can or jar. Use a rubber band to hold the balloon tightly in place.
4. Cut one end of the straw so that it comes to a point. Tape or glue the other end of the straw to the center of the balloon.
5. Put the can or jar next to a wall. Tape a sheet of paper to the wall right behind it. Check the straw over the next few days. See where the pointed tip is. Make a mark on the paper showing how high or low the straw is each day. Does the straw move up or down?

High air pressure pushes the balloon down. Low air pressure lets the balloon rise a little. As air pressure changes, the straw moves up and down. Is the air pressure higher or lower when the straw moves up? What about when it moves down?

See How Cold and Warm Air Move

What you need:
an ice-cube tray
water
blue food coloring
a clear plastic food-storage container (about the size of a shoebox)
red food coloring

What you do:
1. Get an adult to help you.
2. Fill the ice-cube tray with water. Add a drop of blue food coloring to each cube. The blue color will represent cold air. Put the tray into a freezer to make blue ice cubes.
3. Fill the clear plastic container about two-thirds full of water. Let the water sit on a table for about an hour. This will make the water the same temperature as the air in the room.
4. Take the ice cubes out of the tray. Be sure the water in the container is completely still. Carefully slip a blue ice cube into the water at one end of the container. Carefully add two drops of red food coloring to the water at the other end of the container. The red color represents warm air.
5. Watch what happens as the ice cubes melt. Where does the red food coloring go? Where does the blue food coloring go? How is this like what happens when warm and cold air meet?
6. Use more blue ice cubes, fresh water, and red food coloring to do the experiment again. Does the same thing happen every time you add blue ice cubes and red food coloring to the water?

Airy Facts

Fast Air
Streams of air race around the world like rivers in the sky. The fast-moving streams of air are called jet streams. Jet streams are high up. Airplanes can ride on a jet stream. The air in the jet stream makes the planes go faster.

Air and Sound
You can hear because of air. A phone rings. The sound goes out in waves from the phone to your ear. Sound waves are like ripples in a pond. They must have something to ripple through. Sound waves ripple through the air. You cannot see sound waves, but you can hear them.

Where Air Came From
The atmosphere is as old as the earth, but the gases in air have changed since the earth was created. Some gases came out of volcanoes. Oxygen came from plants. Air today is just right for life.

Cloudy Skies
Warm air with lots of water vapor rises up. High up, the air gets colder. In the cold air, the water vapor changes to water droplets. Some droplets freeze into ice crystals and form clouds. When water droplets and ice crystals clump together, they fall from the clouds as rain or snow.

How a Straw Works
Air pressure makes milk go up a straw. When you suck on a straw, you are taking air out of the straw. The pressure outside the straw is greater than it is inside. The higher pressure forces milk up into the straw.

Glossary

air pollution—when harmful materials make air dirty and unsafe

air pressure—the weight of air pushing against something

air resistance—the force of air rubbing against things. Air resistance slows down moving vehicles, such as cars and airplanes.

atmosphere—the gases that surround the earth

carbon dioxide—one of the gases in air. People and animals breathe out carbon dioxide. Plants use it to make food.

oxygen—a gas in air that is important to all plants and animals

water vapor—a gas in the air that is made of water

To Learn More

At the Library

Donald, Rhonda Lucas. *Air Pollution*. New York: Children's Press, 2001.

Hewitt, Sally. *Air*. Brookfield, Conn.: Copper Beech Books, 2003.

Pluckrose, Henry Arthur. *Air*. Milwaukee, Wis.: Gareth Stevens Pub., 2001.

Simon, Seymour. *Let's Try It Out in the Air: Hands-On Early-Learning Science Activities*. New York: Simon & Schuster Books for Young Readers, 2001.

Tocci, Salvatore. *Experiments with Air*. New York: Children's Press, 2002.

On the Web

Fact Hound offers a safe, fun way to find Web sites related to this book. All of the sites on Fact Hound have been researched by our staff.
http://www.facthound.com

1. Visit the Fact Hound home page.
2. Enter a search word related to this book, or type in this special code: 1404802487.
3. Click the FETCH IT button.

Your trusty Fact Hound will fetch the best sites for you!

Index